This *rising moon* book belongs to

APR 0 8

The PLANET HUNTER

The Story Behind
What Happened to Pluto

By ELIZABETH RUSCH   Illustrated by GUY FRANCIS

rising moon

www.risingmoonbooks.com

Composed in the United States of America
Printed in China

Edited by Theresa Howell
Art directed by Sunny H. Yang
Designed by David Alston

FIRST IMPRESSION 2007
ISBN 13: 978-0-87358-926-0
ISBN 10: 0-87358-926-2

07 08 09 10 11   5 4 3 2 1

The author would like to thank Mike Brown—the book would not have been possible without
him—and Christine Pulliam and Chris Isbell for their time in reviewing the book.

Thank you, too, to Johannes Schedler for the use of his photographs.

Library of Congress Cataloging-in-Publication Data

Rusch, Elizabeth.
The planet hunter : The story behind what happened to pluto / by Elizabeth Rusch ;
illustrated by Guy Francis.
p. cm.
ISBN-13: 978-0-87358-926-0 (hardcover)
ISBN-10: 0-87358-926-2 (hardcover)
1. Brown, Mike, 1965---Juvenile literature. 2. Astronomers--United
States--Biography--Juvenile literature. 3. Pluto (Dwarf planet)--Juvenile
literature. I. Francis, Guy, ill. II. Title.
QB36.B89R87 2007
523.2--dc22
2006102043

To Cobi and Izzi:
Seek and ye shall find.
—L.R.

To my brother-in-law, Dallas,
who once went to space camp
—G.F.

ZiNG! SPLaT! SPLaSH!

Mike Brown learned in second grade how meteorites blasted craters on the moon. He ran home after school, made a goopy mud puddle, and winged some rocks sideways at it. He smashed a rock straight down and created a huge crater with spatters along the edges. When he was done, his backyard looked an awful lot like the moon.

Mike grew up in Huntsville, Alabama, home of the Marshall Space Flight Center, where test rockets rumbled the ground. Everyone Mike knew was either a rocket engineer or an astronaut. So, Mike and his brother Andy built model rockets. Andy's flew fine, but Mike's engines sputtered and the fins fell off.

Oh well, thought Mike. But his fascination with outer space lasted his whole life.

To Mike, the night sky was like a friend. Whenever he stepped outside, he looked skyward. When he was in high school, he noticed two really bright stars. He watched all winter as the gleaming stars performed an intricate dance around each other. Then he learned they were not stars at all. They were planets: Jupiter and Saturn!

PLANET LIGHT, PLANET BRIGHT

Some of the stars that shine brightest in the night sky are not stars at all. They are planets. Planets don't make light, like stars, but they reflect light from our star—the sun! The bigger and closer the planet, the brighter the light we see.

Mike often gazed at his poster of the nine planets: Mercury, Venus, Earth, Mars, Jupiter, Saturn, Uranus, Neptune, and Pluto.

He marveled at tiny Pluto, a planet even smaller than our moon. As he traced Pluto's orbit with his finger, he wondered: *Could there be more planets out there?*

Solar System

EARTH

MARS

JUPITER

SATURN

URANUS

NEPTUNE

PLUTO

Kuiper Belt

CALTECH

Mike
Call
Obser
Telescope

When Mike got older and began studying astronomy, a friend discovered something new in our solar system: an object in an area that includes Pluto called the Kuiper (KYE-per) Belt.

"Ohhh, I bet there's more out there," Mike said. "I bet there's another planet."

But how could he find a planet everyone else had missed? Mike remembered how as a kid, he was *always* losing his sneakers. The only way he could be sure to find them was to start at one end of the house and search room by room.

"That's the way to find a planet," he said.

Using an old telescope, Mike began searching the sky, section by section.

One day, a fellow astronomer visited him at the observatory. "What are you looking for?" she asked.

"I think there are other planets in our solar system, and I'm going to find them," Mike said.

"Oh, come on," she said. "You don't really believe that?"

"I can't prove it yet, but I'll bet on it."

So they did. Mike bet that someone would find a new planet—something bigger than Pluto— within four years.

He really hoped it would be him.

SLEEPING ON THE JOB

You'd think planet hunting would mean staying up all night staring into telescopes, right? Wrong! For his planet search, Mike programmed a digital camera on a robotic telescope to take three photos of the same part of the sky over three hours. Computers compare the three photos, searching for any bright object that moves.

Why look for objects that move? From Earth, all the stars and galaxies seem to stand still. Objects in our solar system move.

Mike's clever system can detect objects 10 billion miles away— and all while he's sleeping! "It's a gas," Mike says. "In the morning, I get to see if I found any planets that night!"

Mike searched for two whole years and found nothing.

Then one day, he detected something bright in the Kuiper Belt, out near Pluto. He named the icy object Quaoar (KWAH-o-wahr).

Everyone wanted to know: "Is Quaoar bigger than Pluto?"

Mike shook his head. "Not quite," he said.

FUN FACTS ABOUT QUAOAR

Discovered: 2002

Claim to fame: At the time, the biggest object discovered in the solar system since Pluto.

Looks like: Charon, Pluto's moon.

Size: Same size as Charon. Half the size of Pluto.

Named for: A creation force from the mythology of the San Gabrielino American Indians. Quaoar sings and dances gods into existence.

Weird, weirder, weirdest: It would take you 100,000 years to walk to Quaoar—25 years by space shuttle.

Months went by. Every day, even on weekends, Mike scoured the sky. After another year, he found Sedna, far, far away in a part of the solar system where no one expected to find *anything*.

"Is Sedna bigger than Pluto?" people asked.

"Almost!" Mike replied.

FUN FACTS ABOUT SEDNA

Discovered: 2003

Claim to fame: Found lurking between the Kuiper Belt and the Oort Cloud in a region of the solar system everyone *thought* was basically empty.

Looks like: Mars—Sedna is deep red.

Size: Three-quarters the size of Pluto.

Named for: An Inuit goddess who rules over the sea.

Weird, weirder, weirdest: Sedna's long, oval orbit takes 12,000 Earth years to circle the sun. Astronomers think that soon after our solar system was born, a star passed near enough to tug on Sedna, stretching out its orbit.

FUN FACTS ABOUT SANTA

Discovered: 2004

Claim to fame: Fastest revolving object in the solar system. Revolves end over end every four hours.

Looks like: A squashed football sprayed with a frosting of ice.

Size: As wide as Pluto and half as long.

Named for: That sweet white-bearded guy who wears a red coat and rides a sleigh. Santa is actually a nickname.

Weird, weirder, weirdest: How would you like to have a four-hour day? Time to get up, eat breakfast, eat dinner, bedtime!

Later, Mike discovered a weird object resembling a huge squashed football. He nicknamed this one Santa.

"Is this one bigger than Pluto?" everyone wondered.

Mike shook his head: "Definitely not."

Time was running out. Mike thought: *This is it. I have one month left to find a real planet.*

Instead of taking vacation, Mike spent winter break reviewing all the old photos, searching for objects he had missed.

New Year's Eve was Mike's last
chance. He studied photos all
day long. Nothing. He sighed and
e-mailed his friend: "I guess you won,"
he wrote.

Instead of celebrating the New Year,
Mike went home and went to bed.

But right after New Year's Day, Mike was back at it again. Just five days after losing the bet, Mike flipped through three photos he'd taken of the sky a few months earlier. He stopped and stared hard. There was a slow-moving object, very bright, that he hadn't noticed before.

Can this be right? Mike pushed his glasses up on his nose and checked to make sure he hadn't made a mistake. *How could it be so bright?* His excitement grew: *Bright means big.*

Mike grabbed the phone and dialed his wife: "I think I found a real planet!"

Mike pointed as many telescopes as he could at the light-gray rock, which he named Eris. Floating at the edge of the Kuiper Belt, the shiny ball was smooth and glowed white—like ice.

Mike had to find out: Was Eris so bright because its surface gleamed like snow? Or was it bright because it was big? Was Eris bigger than Pluto? Was Eris the tenth planet?

Finally, photos from the Hubble Space Telescope confirmed it. Eris *was* bigger than Pluto!

FUN FACTS ABOUT ERIS

Discovered: January 5, 2005

Claim to fame: The largest orbiting object since the discovery of Neptune. If Pluto is a planet, so is Eris!

Looks like: A huge shiny ball.

Size: Bigger than Pluto!

Named for: The Greek goddess who stirs up anger and discord.

Weird, weirder, weirdest: In 280 years, Eris will swing closer to the sun, and its frozen atmosphere may melt, giving it a whole new look!

Mike's discovery caused an uproar. Astronomers around the globe asked: What is a planet anyway? If tiny Eris and Pluto are planets, why not Sedna and Quaoar? Why not all the round, orbiting objects recently discovered in our solar system?

But to Mike, that wouldn't make sense. By the time his daughter Lilah would be old enough to memorize the planets, there could be hundreds!

What do my discoveries really mean? Mike asked himself. Perhaps astronomers were wrong to call Pluto a planet in the first place. After all, Pluto's so much smaller than the other planets. And it floats near Eris and Quaoar and a bunch of other objects just like it.

Even scientists make mistakes, Mike thought.

ROUND-UP!

What makes a space blob round? It helps to know how planets are formed. It all starts with a dense mass of material that pulls other rubble toward itself. When the whirling mass has enough gravity, it forms a pile. When the pile becomes big enough—at least 250 miles across— its gravity pulls all the material into a round shape. Now that's a round-up!

Astronomers from around the globe gathered to decide once and for all what a planet really is.

Mike held his breath.

With a flash of yellow voting cards, it was settled: A planet is a body that circles the sun. It's large enough to be round. And it orbits alone, far from anything else its size.

HEY YOU, GET OFF OF MY ORBIT!

In the solar system, big objects boss smaller objects around. The gravity of huge objects tugs smaller stuff toward itself. Some small objects crash in, like meteorites. Some are pulled into a close orbit and become moons. Finally, gravity from several massive objects can bump other objects out of the way—even all the way out of the solar system!

See ya later alligator!

None of Mike's discoveries were considered planets.
Not even Pluto was a planet any more. Every single
book, poster, and placemat picturing the solar system
had to be changed. But Mike smiled. Astronomers had
fixed a mistake. Science had progressed!

And the Planet Hunter's search has just begun. Now, Mike Brown is searching even farther into our solar system, out toward the Oort Cloud, where Sedna soars. Once again, Mike wonders: *Is there more out there?*

Maybe a real planet, something bigger than Mercury or even Earth, floats all by itself. That would *really* shake up our solar system.

"No one expects it to be out there," Mike says.

"But it will be. I just know it."

EPILOGUE
PLANET SEARCH: THE NEXT GENERATION

Mike Brown has surveyed half of the sky—the amount visible from the northern hemisphere out to about eight times past Pluto. His new survey will explore farther—out to twenty times past Pluto. And someone, somewhere will probably explore the sky from the southern hemisphere. But today's technology can't clearly see the Oort Cloud or other rocky planets in other solar systems. That's work left for you, the next generation of

PLANET HUNTERS!

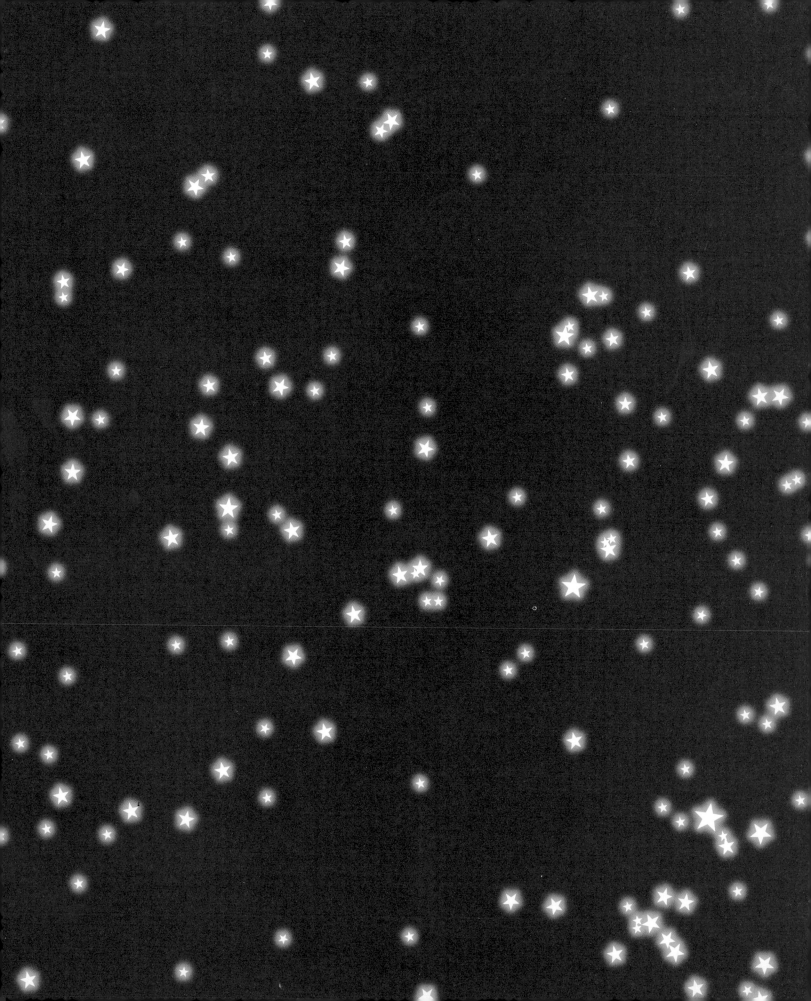